C000156763

1,000,000 Books

are available to read at

www.ForgottenBooks.com

Read online
Download PDF
Purchase in print

ISBN 978-1-5276-2980-6
PIBN 10046589

This book is a reproduction of an important historical work. Forgotten Books uses state-of-the-art technology to digitally reconstruct the work, preserving the original format whilst repairing imperfections present in the aged copy. In rare cases, an imperfection in the original, such as a blemish or missing page, may be replicated in our edition. We do, however, repair the vast majority of imperfections successfully; any imperfections that remain are intentionally left to preserve the state of such historical works.

Forgotten Books is a registered trademark of FB &c Ltd.
Copyright © 2018 FB &c Ltd.
FB &c Ltd, Dalton House, 60 Windsor Avenue, London, SW19 2RR.
Company number 08720141. Registered in England and Wales.

For support please visit www.forgottenbooks.com

1 MONTH OF
FREE
READING

at

www.ForgottenBooks.com

By purchasing this book you are eligible for one month membership to ForgottenBooks.com, giving you unlimited access to our entire collection of over 1,000,000 titles via our web site and mobile apps.

To claim your free month visit:

www.forgottenbooks.com/free46589

* Offer is valid for 45 days from date of purchase. Terms and conditions apply.

English
Français
Deutsche
Italiano
Español
Português

www.forgottenbooks.com

Mythology Photography **Fiction**
Fishing Christianity **Art** Cooking
Essays Buddhism Freemasonry
Medicine **Biology** Music **Ancient
Egypt** Evolution Carpentry Physics
Dance Geology **Mathematics** Fitness
Shakespeare **Folklore** Yoga Marketing
Confidence Immortality Biographies
Poetry **Psychology** Witchcraft
Electronics Chemistry History **Law**
Accounting **Philosophy** Anthropology
Alchemy Drama Quantum Mechanics
Atheism Sexual Health **Ancient History**
Entrepreneurship Languages Sport
Paleontology Needlework Islam
Metaphysics Investment Archaeology
Parenting Statistics Criminology
Motivational

AN

ACCOUNT

OF THE

Revival of Religion in Boston,

IN THE YEARS 1740–1–2–3.

....

BY THOMAS PRINCE,
One of the then Pastors of the Old South Church.

....

"We have heard with our ears, O God! our fathers have told us, what work thou didst in their days, in the times of old.—Psalm xliv, 1."
"Thus saith the Lord, stand ye in the ways, and see, and ask for the old paths, where is the good way and walk therein, and ye shall find rest for your souls.—Jeremiah vi, 16."

—

BOSTON:
REPUBLISHED BY SAMUEL T. ARMSTRONG, 50, CORNHILL.
Crocker & Brewster, Printers.
1823.

US 13175.7

HARVARD
UNIVERSITY
LIBRARY
JAN 4 1960

ADVERTISEMENT.

Presuming that it would be highly gratifying to man
present day, to be made acquainted with the views of ou
on the subject of Revivals of Religion, the followin
from "the learned and judicious Mr. Prince," is now
and submitted to the Christian Public, with the hope, th
be attended with the blessing of Almighty God, and con
the promotion of "pure and undefiled religion."

ACCOUNT, &c.

IT is, I hope, for the glory of God and the public good, that I have drawn up the following Narrative of the late Revival of Religion here, according to the best of my remembrance.

And that the grace and power of God may appear the more illustrious, it seems fit to give a brief and previous history of the general state of religion here, even from my returning hither in 1717, after above eight years travelling abroad, to the time of this revival at the end of 1740.

On my said return, there were five Congregational churches settled with pastors in this town; though now they are increased to five more. The pastors were Dr. Increase and Cotton Mather of the North Church; Mr. Wadsworth, with Mr. Foxcroft, chosen his colleague of the Old Church; Mr. Colman and Cooper of the Church in Brattle-street; Mr. Sewall of the South Church; and Mr. Webb of the New North All most happily agreeing in the doctrines of grace, as laid down in the shorter and larger Catechisms and Confession of Faith, drawn out of Scripture by the venerable Assembly of Divines at West-minister, as well as the Confession of Faith agreed to by our New-England Synods, and almost the same with the other. And this town and country were in great tran-quillity both civil and religious. But though there were

many bright examples of piety in every seat a
yet there was a general complaint among the
elderly persons, of the great decay of godline
lives and conversations of people both in the t
land, from what they had seen in the days of their
There was scarce a prayer made in public by t
ministers without some heavy lamentation of th
in their sermons also they frequently mourne
the younger ministers commonly followed their ex
therein.

Soon after my arrival I was called to preach t
South Church: and in 1718, ordained their co-pasto
my dear class-mate the Rev. Mr. Sewall, who had
ordained to that office about five years before.

In the spring of 1721, the eight ministers who c
on the public Lecture, taking into consideration tl
mentable defect of piety among our young people, a
to preach a Course of Sermons at the Lecture to
The audiences were considerably crowded: and whi
word of God was loudly sounding, he lifted up his
rod, by sending the small-pox into the town, which be
to spread to our general consternation: scarce a quar
of the people being thought to have had it; and none
the numerous youth under eighteen years of age; it bei
so many years since that fatal pestilence had prevail
among us. The sermons were quickly printed, with
other added by the venerable Dr. Increase Mather,
further benefit. Many of the younger people especia
were then greatly awakened: and many hundreds of th
quickly after swept into eternity.

In the spring of 1722, the distemper left us: but so
tle reformed were the surviving youth, that at the end
the summer, the pastors agreed to move their church
to keep in each successively "a day of prayer and fastir
to ask of God the effusion of his Holy Spirit, particula
on the rising generation." And the churches readily
ceived the motion.

But though a solemnity appeared on many, yet
pleased the holy God to humble us and sparingly to gi
the blessing.

And though in the spring of 1726, in an awakenir
view of the deplorable decay of family religion, as
principal source of all other decays, the pastors went in
a course of Public Lectures on that important subject; y

they had the further sorrow to see those Lectures too thinly attended to expect much benefit from them.*

But after all our endeavors, both our security and degeneracy seemed in general to grow, until the night after the Lord's Day, October 29, 1727; when the glorious God arose and fearfully shook the earth through all these countries. By terrible things in righteousness He began to answer us, as the God of our salvation.

On the next morning a very full assembly met at the North Church, for the proper exercises on so extraordinary an occasion. At five in the evening a crowded concourse assembled at the Old Church: and multitudes unable to get in, immediately flowed to the South, and in a few minutes filled that also. At lieutenant-governor Dummer's motion, (who was then our Commander-in-Chief,) the Thursday of the same week was kept as a day of *extraordinary fasting and prayer* in all the churches in Boston; not merely to intreat for sparing mercy, but also to implore the grace and Spirit of God to come down and help us to a sincere repentance and returning to him. And as the houses of public worship were greatly crowded, the people were very attentive.

The ministers endeavored to set in with this extraordinary and awakening work of God in nature, and to preach his word in the most awakening manner; to show the people the vast difference between conviction and conversion, between a forced reformation either in acts of piety, justice, charity, or sobriety, by the mere power of fear, and a genuine change of the very frame and relish of the heart by the supernatural efficacy of the Holy Spirit; to lead them on to true conversion and unfeigned faith in Christ, and to guard them against deceiving themselves.

In all our congregations, many seemed to be awakened and reformed: and professing repentance of their sins

* The several subjects were these:—Dr. C. Mather, Job viii, 6, on househould piety in general. Mr Colman, 2 Sam. vi, 20, on family worship. Mr. Thacher, Gen. xviii, 19, on family instruction. Mr. Sewall, 1 Sam iii, 13, on family government. Mr. Prince, Lev. xxiii, 3, on family sabbatizing. Mr. Webb, Psalm ci, 2, on family example. Mr. Cooper, Ezekiel xvi, 20, on improving the covenant relating to children. Mr. Foxcroft, Col. iii, 18, 19, on conjugal duties. Mr. Checkley, Col. iii, 20, 22—24, on the duties of children and servants. Mr. Waldron, Prov. xiv, 11, the character and doom of wicked houses. Mr. Gee, Eccl. vii, 14, family Providences, especially afflictive, improved.

1*

and faith in Christ, entered into solemn covenant f r
God, and came into full communion with our sev
churches. In ours, within eight months after, were at
eighty added to our communicants. But then comp:
tively few of these applied to me to discourse about tl
souls until they came to offer themselves to the Comm
ion, or afterwards: the most of those who came to
seemed to have passed through their convictions bel
their coming to converse with me about approaching
the Lord's Table: though I doubt not but considert
numbers were at that time savingly converted.

However the goodness of many seemed as the morr
cloud and early dew which quickly passes away. A s
itual slumber seemed soon to seize the generality; e
the wise as well as foolish virgins. And though in 1'
the small pox came into town and prevailed again; ye
a few months left us, both unawakened, ungrateful,
reformed. The Holy Spirit awfully withheld his ir
ence in convincing and converting sinners, and enlivei
others. In three or four years we rather grew 1
greater declension than ever: and so alarmed were
pastors of the town with the dismal view, that in the s
mer of 1734, they agreed to propose another Cours
Days of Prayer and Fasting among our several congreg
tions: "To humble ourselves before God for our unfrui
fulness under the means of grace, and to ask the effusio
of his Spirit to revive the power of godliness among us
which our people readily complied with and observed.

And though the sovereign God was pleased to give
now and then a sprinkling, for which His name be praise
yet the parching drought continued, and He made us wait
for a larger effusion.

In this year the terrible throat-distemper broke o
and spread among the youth in the easterly parts of th
country, and destroyed multitudes. In some towns it cu
off almost all the children. The next year it came into
Boston, and began to destroy and strike us with a general
awe: but gently treated us, and the next year left us; t
melt our hearts into a grateful repentance. And yet we
generally seemed to grow more stupid and hard than ever

About this time indeed, viz. 1735, there was a mos
remarkable revival of religion in the westerly parts o
the country: not only at Northampton, but also in abou
twelve other congregations in the county of Hampshire

l in about fourteen others in the neighboring colony of
nnecticut. And the solemn rumor of that surprising
rk of God resounding through the country, was a
cial. means of exciting great thoughtfulness of heart
nany irreligious people; and great joy in others, both
he view of what the mighty power and grace of God
l wrought, and in the hopeful prospect that this bless-
work begun would go on and spread throughout the
d. And as this excited the extraordinary prayers of
ny, so it seemed to prepare the way in divers places
that more extensive revival of religion which in five
irs after followed. But, in the mean while, the general
:ay of piety seemed to increase among us in Boston.
d for the congregation I preach to; though for several
irs some few offered themselves to our Communion,
: but few came to me in concern about their souls be-
e. And so I perceive it was in others: and I remember
ne of the ministers were wont to express themselves
greatly discouraged with the growing declension both
principle and practice, especially among the rising
neration. From the year 1738, we had received ac-
ints of the Rev. Mr. Whitefield, as a very pious young
nister of the Church of England, rising up in the spirit
the Reformers, and preaching their doctrines first in
gland and then in America, with surprising power and
cess: which raised desires in great numbers among us
see and hear him. And having received invitations to
ne hither; he, from Georgia and South-Carolina, ar-
ed at Rhode-Island, on Lord's Day, Sept. 14, 1740, and
: Thursday evening after came to Boston.
Next day, in the afternoon, Dr. Sewall and I made him
isit: found several ministers and other gentlemen of
: town with him, and that Dr. Colman and Mr. Cooper
l engaged him to preach in the afternoon in their House
public worship: and in about an hour we went to
: place, which quickly crowded with two or three
usand people. He began with a short and fervent
iyer: and after singing, took his text from John xvii,
Gave us a plain, weighty, regular discourse: repre-
iting that all our learning and morality will never save
and without an experimental knowledge of God in
rist, we must perish in hell for ever. He spake as
:ame the oracles of God in demonstration of the Spirit
l of power. And especially when he came to his ap-

public and moving manner observed to the people, how sorry he was to hear that the religious assemblies, espepecially on lectures, had been so thin, exhorted them earnestly to a more general attendance on our public ministrations for the time to come, and told them how glad he should be to hear of the same.

Multitudes were greatly affected and many awakened with his lively ministry. Though he preached every day, the houses were exceedingly crowded: but when he preached in the common, a vaster number attended: and almost every evening the house where he lodged was thronged, to hear his prayers and counsels.

Upon invitation he also preached in several neighboring towns; travelled and preached as far as York, above sevently miles northeast of Boston; returned hither; gave us his farewell affectionate sermon, Lord's Day evening, October 12. Next morning left us; travelled westward to Northampton; thence through Connecticut, New York and New Jersey, to Philadelphia, and thence sailed to South Carolina. And as far as I could then see or learn, he parted in the general esteem and love both of ministers and people: and this seemed to continue until the Journal of his Travels in New England came abroad, wherein some passages offended many, and occasioned their reflections on him.

But upon Mr. Whitefield's leaving us, great numbers in this town were so happily concerned about their souls, as we had never seen any thing like it before, except at the time of the general earthquake:* and their desires excited to hear their ministers more than ever: so that our assemblies both on Lectures and Sabbaths were surprisingly increased, and now the people wanted to hear us oftener. In consideration of which, a public Lecture was proposed to be set up at Dr. Colman's church, near the midst of the town, on every Tuesday evening.

Lord's Day afternoon, October 19, public notice was there given of the proposed Lecture to be on the Tues-

*Though people were then generally frighted and many awakened to such a sense of their duty as to offer themselves to our Communion; yet very few came to me then under deep convictions of their unconverted and lost condition, in comparison of what came now. Nor did those who came to me then, come so much with the inquiry, What shall we do to be saved? as to signify they had such a sense of their duty to come to the Lord's Table, that they dare not stay away any longer.

day evening following: which the religious peop[l]
general received with so much joy, that when th[e] [e]
ing came, the house seemed to be crowded as muc[h]
Mr. Whitefield was there. It was the first stated e[ver]
Lecture in these parts of the. world: and the ve[n]er[i]
Dr. Colman began it with a most suitable and [m]o[r]
sermon; forthwith printed. The title whereof is this
  "Souls flying to Jesus Christ, pleasant and admir[e]
to behold. A Sermon preached at the opening o[f]
Evening Lecture in Brattle-street, Boston, Tuesday,
[Oc]tober 21, 1740: by Dr. Colman: to a very crowded a[s]
[s]ence: and printed at the desire of many."

And thus the Dr. began the sermon:—
"Isaiah lx, 8. *Who are these that fly as a cloud, an[d]
the doves to their windows?*
  "It is a pleasant and wondrous thing, to see souls fl[y]
to Jesus Christ, to the means of grace and salva
which he has ordained and sanctified, and into his chu[rch]
If this were not the proper and natural sense of the [pro]
phet's words, I would not have chose them for the o[pen]
ing of the present Lecture.

"Our dear people, your ministers have with plea[se]
seen you in the weeks past, old and young, parents
children, masters and servants, high and low, rich a[nd]
poor together, gathering and passing as clouds in o[ur]
streets, and as doves on the wing in flocks flying to th[e]
doors and windows of our places of worship; and hoverin[g]
about the same, those that could not get in.

"The fame of a singular fervent and holy youth, an[d]
extraordinary servant and minister of Jesus Christ, (wh[o]
makes his angels spirits, and his ministers a flame of fire,)
had prepared you for his visit; and with raised expecta[
tions we received him, even as an angel of God for Jesus'
sake; as the apostle St. Paul was received by the churche[s]
in Galatia.

"God gave him a wonderful manner of entrance among
us, just as in other places before us, among the brethre[n]
of our denomination; and we were sometimes melted together in tears, ministers and people, parents and children, under the commanding addresses of love to his Savior and our souls. We led you with a visible pleasure i[n]
our faces to the solemn and great assemblies, and looke[d]
on you there with great satisfaction, in your uncommon
regards to the beloved servant of Christ, for the truth'[s]

sake that dwelleth in him, and the love of the Spirit filling him, and reigning in his ministrations to us.

"And now our beloved brethren and sisters, you and your children, we are going to prove, confirm and increase, by the will of God, the seeming good dispositions begun or revived in you, toward Christ and his word, in a just and reasonable pious care and solicitude for your salvation.

"Mr. Whitefield once and again in his admonitions to you, and also in his fervent, righteous and effectual prayers for you (by the will of God) led you into this trial and proof of yourselves; Whether when he was gone from us, you would better attend on the ministry of your own pastors, both on Sabbaths and Lectures? For he had heard (and it was but too true) that there had been a very great defect in this point among you before he came. Some of your ministers therefore now make a new tender of themselves to you, in the fear and love of God, in this new Lecture, for the service of your souls, if you will encourage them by something of a like attendance on it, as we have lately seen you give to the word preached. We preach the same Christ, the same doctrines of grace, and according to godliness, with the same gospel motives and arguments, applications to conscience, and supplications to God for you. We would look on the fields, and behold them white for the harvest, and desire to enter into it; if by the help of God we may cherish the impressions made on any of your souls, and carry them on, clinching the nails driven by the master of assemblies that has been sent among us. For though we are elder ministers, and have been many years before him in the service of souls, and he like David going against Goliath, in the sight of the armies of Israel, has been seen to be but a youth and stripling; yet are we not unwilling or ashamed to come and serve after him, in the battles of our Lord, and in the victories of his grace. You have seen, as it were, a young Elias, or the Baptist risen again, a burning and a shining light, and you were willing for the season to rejoice in his light and heat: may we now preach and you hear for the future, with more life and spirit, diligence and constancy; and by the will of God with new success. But we mean not, brethren, at this Lecture only, but on every Sabbath and every Lecture in the town; and more particularly on the public Thursday Lecture; which has been shamefully neglected the town.

"To come then to my text, which I acknowledge late concourse to the word among us, has led m choose. I would now look round on the present as bly, and look back on our past assemblies, and say to *Who are these that fly as a cloud, and as the doves to windows?*"

The Tuesday evening after, the Rev. Dr. Se preached the Lecture in the same place; and the h was then also greatly crowded with attentive hea and so it continued to be on these Lectures for n months after.

Upon the Rev. Mr. Gilbert Tennent's coming preaching here, the people appeared to be yet r more awakened about their souls than before. He c I think, on Saturday, December 13, this year: prea at the New North on both the parts of the following as also on Monday in the afternoon, when I first h him, and there was a great assembly.

He did not indeed at first come up to my expects but afterwards exceeded it. In private converse him, I found him to be a man of considerable parts learning; free, gentle, condescending: and from his various experience, reading the most noted writers experimental divinity, as well as the Scriptures, and co versing with many who had been awakened by his mi istry in New Jersey, where he then lived; he seemed t have as deep an acquaintance with the experimental pa of religion as any I have conversed with; and his preach ing was as searching and rousing as ever I heard.

He seemed to have no regard to please the eyes of h hearers with agreeable gesture, nor their ears with de livery, nor their fancy with language; but to aim d rectly at their hearts and consciences, to lay open the ruinous delusions, shew them their numerous, secre hypocritical shifts in religion, and drive them out of ever deceitful refuge wherein they made themselves ea with the form of godliness without the power. A many who were pleased in a good conceit of themselv before, now found, to their great distress, they were on self-deceived hypocrites. And though while the disco ery was making, some at first raged, as they have own to me and others; yet in the progress of the discove many were forced to submit; and then the power of God so broke and humbled them, that they wanted a further and even a thorough discovery; they went to hear him, that the secret corruptions and delusions of their hearts might be more discovered; and the more searching the sermon, the more acceptable it was to their anxious minds.

From the terrible and deep convictions he had passed through in his own soul, he seemed to have such a lively view of the divine Majesty, the spirituality, purity, extensiveness, and strictness of his law; with his glorious holiness, and displeasure at sin, his justice, truth, and power in punishing the damned; that the very terrors of God seemed to rise in his mind afresh, when he displayed and brandished them in the eyes of unreconciled sinners. And though some could not bear the representation, and avoided his preaching; yet the arrows of conviction, by his ministry, seemed so deeply to pierce the hearts of others, and even some of the most stubborn sinners, as to make them fall down at the feet of Christ, and yield a lowly submission to him.

And here I cannot but observe, that those who call these convictions by the name of religious frights or fears, and then ascribe them to the mere natural or mechanical influence of terrible words, sounds and gestures, moving tones, or boisterous ways of speaking, appear to me to be not sufficiently acquainted with the subjects of this work, as carried on in the town in general, or with the nature of their convictions; or at least as carried on among the people I have conversed with. For I have had awakened people of every assembly of the Congregational and Presbyterian way in town, in considerable numbers repairing to me from time to time; and from their various and repeated narratives shall show the difference.

I don't remember any crying out, or falling down, or fainting, either under Mr. Whitefield's or Mr. Tennent's ministry all the while they were here; though many, both women and men, both those who had been vicious, and those who had been moral, yea, some religious and learned, as well as unlearned, were in great concern of soul. But as Dr. Colman well expressed it in his Letter of November 23, 1741. "We have seen little of those extremes or supposed blemishes of this work in Boston, but much of the blessed fruits of it have fallen to our

share. God has spoken to us in a more soft and gentle
wind; and we have neither had those outcries and f
ings in our assemblies, which have disturbed the wor
in many places; nor yet those manifestations of joy
expressible, which now fill some of our eastern parts.

As to Mr. Whitefield's preaching—it was, in the n
ner, moving, earnest, winning, melting: but the mecl
ical influence of this, according to the usual operatior
mechanical powers, in two or three days expired; v
many, in two or three hours; and I believe with the m
as soon as the sound was over, or they got out of
house, or in the first conversation they fell into.
with the manner of his preaching, wherein he appea
to be in earnest, he delivered those vital truths wl
animated all our martyrs, made them triumph in flan
and led his hearers into the view of that vital, inward,
tive piety, which is the mere effect of the mighty
supernatural operation of a divine Power on the souls
men; which only will support and carry through
sharpest trials, and make meet for the inheritance of
saints in light. His chief and earnest desires and lab
appeared to be the same with the apostle Paul for th
visible saints at Ephesus; viz. that they might know (i. e
by experience) what is the exceeding greatness of hi
power (i. e. the power of God) to us-ward who believe
according to the working of his mighty power which he
wrought in Christ when he raised him from the dead.—
Eph. i. And they were these things, and this sort of
preaching with surprising fervency, that the Holy Spirit
was pleased to use as means to make many sensible they
knew nothing of these mighty operations, nor of these
vital principles within them; but that with Simon Magus,
who was a visible believer and professor of Christ and his
religion, they were in "the gall of bitterness and in the
bonds of iniquity;" i. e. in the state, pollution, guilt and
power of sin, which is inexpressibly more disagreeable to
the holy God than the most bitter gall to men, and will be
bitterness to them, without a mighty change, in the latter
end.

It was by such means as these, that the Holy Spirit
seized and awakened the consciences of many; and when
the mechanical influence on the animal passions ceased,
still continued these convictions, not only for many days,
but weeks and months after the sound was over; yea, to

very day with some; while they excited others to an
est and persevering application to Jesus for his Spirit
uicken them, till they came to an hopeful perception
is quickening influence in them; and while in others
sovereign and offended Spirit leaving off to strive,
e convictions in their consciences, the effects thereof,
e either sooner or later died away.

s to Mr. Tennent's preaching—It was frequently
terrible and searching. It was often for matter
y terrible, as he, according to the inspired oracles,
bited the dreadful holiness, justice, law, threatenings,
n, power, majesty of God; and His anger with rebel-
s, impenitent, unbelieving and Christless sinners; the
il danger they were every moment in of being struck
n to hell, and being damned for ever; with the amaz-
niseries of that place of torment. But his exhibitions,
for matter and manner, fell inconceivably below the
ity: and though this terrible preaching may strongly
k on the natural passions and frighten the hearers,
e the soul, and prepare the way for terrible convic-
s; yet those mere natural terrors, and these convic-
s are quite different things.

othing is more obvious than for people to be greatly
ified with the apprehensions of God, eternity and
, and yet have no convictions.

Old England and New, where I have been a constant
cher and an observer of the religious state of those
heard me, for above thirty years, many have passed
er scores of most dreadful tempests of thunder and
tning: wherein, as the Psalmist represents, "the voice
ie Lord was upon the waters, the God of glory thun-
d, the voice of the Lord was powerful, the voice of
Lord was full of majesty; the voice of the Lord broke
cedars, divided the flames of fire, shook the wilder-
, and (in the darkest night) discovered the forests."
, even since the Revival, viz. on Friday night, July
1742, at the Lecture in the South Church, near nine
ck, being very dark, there came on a very terrible
n of thunder and lightning: and just as the blessing
given, an amazing clap broke over the church with
cing repetitions, which set many a shrieking, and the
le assembly into great consternation: God then ap-
ed "terrible out of His high places; they heard at-
vely the noise of His voice, and the sound that went

out of his mouth; He directed it under the whole l
and His lightning to the ends of the earth; after it
roared, He thundered marvellously with his voice:
this the hearts of many (as Elihu's) trembled, an
moved out of their places," for near two hours to
And yet in all these displays of the majesty of G
terrifying apprehensions of danger of sudden destr
neither in this surprising night, nor in all the co
thirty years have I scarce known any, by these kind
terrors brought under genuine convictions. And w
minister has a voice like God, and who can thunder
Him?

So on Lord's day, June 3d last, in our time of pu
worship in the forenoon, when we had been abo
quarter of an hour in prayer, the mighty power of (
came on with a surprising roar and earthquake; wl
made the house with all the galleries to rock and trem
with such a grating noise as if the bricks were mo
out of their places to come down and bury us: wh
exceedingly disturbed the congregation, excited
shrieks of many, put many on flying out, and the ge
ality in motion. But though many were greatly terrif
yet in a day or two their terrors seemed to vanish, a
know of but two or three seized by convictions on
awful occasion.

No! conviction is quite another sort of a thing. I
the work of the Spirit of God, a sovereign, free and
mighty agent; wherein He gives the sinful soul such
clear and lively view of the glory of the Divine So
reignty, omnipresence, holiness, justice, truth and pow
the extensiveness, spirituality and strictness of His law;
binding nature, efficacy and dreadfulness of His curs
the multitude and heinousness of its sins both of comn
sion and omission; the horrible vileness, wickedness, p
verseness and hypocrisy of the heart, with its utter im
tence either rightly to repent, or believe in Christ,
change itself: so that it sees itself in a lost, undone an
perishing state; without the least degree of worthines
to recommend it to the holy and righteous God, and the
least degree of strength to help itself out of this condition. These discoveries are made by means of some re-
vealed truths, either in the reading, hearing or remembrance: when in the hearing, sometimes by words of terror, and sometimes by words of tenderness: and the holy

Spirit with such internal evidence and power so applies them to the conscience, that they become as sharp arrows piercing into the heart, wounding, paining and sticking in it, when all the mechanical impressions of frightful sounds are over, sometimes for many days, weeks and months, if not years together; until this Divine Agent, by these and other convictions, agreeable to His inspired word, entirely subdues the soul to Christ; or being ungratefully treated, withdraws His convincing influence, and leaves the heart and conscience to greater and more dangerous hardness and stupidity than ever.

Such were the convictions wrought in many hundreds in this town by Mr. Tennent's searching ministry: and such was the case of those many scores of several other congregations as well as mine, who came to me and others for direction under them.* And indeed by all their converse I found, it was not so much the terror, as the searching nature of his ministry, that was the principal means of their conviction. It was not merely, nor so much his laying open the terrors of the law and wrath of God, or damnation of hell; (for this they could pretty well bear, as long as they hoped these belonged not to them, or they could easily avoid them;) as his laying open their many vain and secret shifts and refuges, counterfeit resemblances of grace, delusive and damning hopes, their utter impotence, and impending danger of destruction: whereby they found all their hopes and refuges of lies to fail them, and themselves exposed to eternal ruin, unable to help themselves, and in a lost condition. This searching preaching was both the suitable and principal means of their conviction: though it is most evident, the most proper means are utterly insufficient; and wholly depend on the sovereign will of God, to put forth His power and apply them by this or that instrument, on this or that person, at this or that season, in this or that way or manner; with these or those permitted circumstances, infirmities, corruptions, errors, agencies, oppositions; and to what degree, duration and event He pleases.

* The same kind of searching preaching by our own ministers and others, I also observed was the most successful means of bringing people into powerful convictions, or clear and awakening views of their sinful and lost condition, and their absolute need of Christ to find and save them.

2*

A remarkable instance of conviction also,
sometimes under the ministry of the Rev. Mr. E
Northampton: a preacher of a low and moderat
natural way of delivery; and without any ag
body, or any thing else in the manner to excite
except his habitual and great solemnity, looki
speaking as in the presence of God, and with a w
sense of the matter delivered. And on the othe
I have known several very worthy ministers of lc
rousing voices; and yet to their great sorrow the
ality of their people, for a long course of years as
deep security. It is just as the Holy Spirit ple
hide occasions of pride from man: and if Mr. Tenne
to come here again and preach more rousingly tha
it may be, not one soul would come under convic
him.

On Monday, March 2, 1740-1, Mr. Tennent pr
his farewell sermon to the people of Boston, from
23, to an auditory extremely crowded, very attenti
much affected, in Dr. Colman's house of worship.
an affectionate parting, and as great numbers of all
tions and ages appeared awakened by him, there s
to be a general sadness at his going away.

Though it was natural for them to resort abun
to him by whom it pleased the sovereign God chi
awaken them, for advice in their soul concerr
while he was here, many repaired to their ministei
and many more and oftener when he was gone.
Tennent's ministry, with the various cases of tho
sorting to us, excited us to treat more largely
workings of the Spirit of grace, as a Spirit of convict
and conversion, consolation and edification in the soul
men, agreeable to the holy Scriptures, and the comn
experiences of true believers.

And now was such a time as we never knew. T
Rev. Mr. Cooper was won't to say, that more came
him in one week in deep concern about their souls, tl
in the whole twenty-four years of his preceding minist
I can also say the same as to the numbers who repail
to me. By Mr. Cooper's Letter to his friend in Scotla
it appears, he has had about six hundred different pers
in three months time: and Mr. Webb informs me, he l
had in the same space above a thousand.

Agreeable to the numerous bills of the awakened
up in public, sometimes rising to the number of sixty

once, there repaired to us both boys and girls, young men and women, Indians and negroes, heads of families, aged persons; those who had been in full communion and going on in a course of religion many years. And their cases represented were; a blind mind, a vile and hard heart, and some under a deep sense thereof; some under great temptations; some in great concern for their souls; some in great distress of mind for fear of being unconverted; others for fear they had been all along building on a righteousness of their own, and were still in the gall of bitterness and bond of iniquity. Some under slight, others under strong convictions of their sins and sinfulness, guilt and condemnation, the wrath and curse of God upon them, their impotence and misery; some for a long time, even for several months under these convictions: some fearing lest the Holy Spirit should withdraw; others having quenched His operations, were in great distress lest He should leave them for ever: persons far advanced in years afraid of being left behind, while others were hastening to the great Redeemer.

Nor were the same persons satisfied with coming once or twice, as formerly, but again and again, I know not how often; complaining of their evil and cursed hearts; of their past and present unbelief, pride, hypocrisy, perfidiousness, contempt of Christ and God, and alienation from them, their love and captivity to sin, and utter impotence to help themselves, or even to believe on Christ, &c. renouncing every degree of worthiness in and utterly condemning themselves; greatly afraid of deceiving their own souls; and earnestly desirous of being searched, discovered and shown the true way of salvation.

Both people and ministers seemed under a divine influence to quicken each other. The people seemed to have a renewed taste for those old pious and experimental writers, Mr. Hooker, Shepard, Gurnal, William Guthrie, Joseph Alein, Isaac Ambrose, Dr. Owen, and others; as well as later—such as Mr. Mead, Flavel, Shaw, Willard, Stoddard, Dr. Increase and Cotton Mather, Mr. Mather of Windsor, Mr. Boston, &c. The evangelical writings of these deceased authors, as well as of others alive, both in England, Scotland and New England, were now read with singular pleasure; some of them reprinted and in great numbers quickly bought and studied. And the more experimental our preaching was, like theirs, the more it was relished.

The people seemed to love to hear us more than
the weekly Tuesday evening Lectures at the Chur
Brattle-street, were much crowded and not suffi
April 17, 1741, another Lecture was therefore o[
every Friday evening at the South Church; when a
sonable discourse was given by the Rev. Dr. Sewall,
Job xvi, 8: and soon after, another Lecture every '
day and Friday evening was opened at the New N
three of the most capacious houses of public worsh
town; the least of which I suppose will hold three
sand people.   Besides the ancient Lecture every T
day noon, at the Old Church; and other Lectures in (
churches.

Dr. Sewall's discourse, with three other excellen[
mons on the same text, were soon after published
the first of which he says, page 20, "As more lately,
have received good news of this kind from more dist
places upon this continent; so I cannot but hope t[
God's sending one and another of his servants among
who had been personally acquainted with these later w[
derful works of grace, together with their very laborio[
and fervent preaching, and the ministry of others his s[
vants; has been blessed to convince many of their si[
and awaken them to a serious concern about their soul[
Yea, it is hopeful that there are a number converted[
and brought home to Christ.   Let us give the praise t[
the God of all grace."   In the second, he says, page 66
"To conclude, let us with humble thankfulness behol[
that remarkable work of grace which I trust God is carrying on in this town and other places; and be encouraged
to seek the Lord more earnestly, that His kingdom may
come with power by the more plentiful effusions of Hi[
holy Spirit; and that the Lord would rebuke Satan in al[
his attempts to hinder or reproach this work, and bruise
him under our feet.   Let us bless God for his Spirit and
grace manifested in and with his servants that have
preached the gospel among us, and for the great succes[
which has attended their painful labors."   In the fourth,
he says, page last, "And let such as are under good impressions from the Spirit, take heed to themselves, and
beware of apostasy. O ponder those awful words! 'I[
any man draw back, my soul shall have no pleasure in
him,' Heb. x, 38.   But if there should come a falling
away respecting some that have promised fair, let us no[

be shaken in mind as if the main work was not of God; nor take up an evil report against it. Scripture and experience warn us to fear and prepare for such a trial."

And in the Preface he says, "It hath pleased the sovereign and gracious God, in whose hand our times are, to ordain that we should live under some peculiar advantages for our precious souls. For to the ordinary means, we have super-added the manifestation of the Spirit, in extraordinary works of grace. We have lately heard glad tidings from one place and another, that many are inquiring the way to Zion, with their faces thitherward; and some are declaring what God hath done for their souls. Yea, God hath brought this work home to our own doors, and we hear many crying out, 'What must we do to be saved!' And there are a number hopefully rejoicing in God's salvation. Of such a season as this it may well be said, 'I have heard thee in a time accepted, and in the day of salvation have I succoured thee: behold, now is the accepted time; behold, now is the day of salvation.' I hope God's people are reaping the fruit of their prayers, particularly on extraordinary days of fasting observed with an especial view to this great blessing, the plentiful effusion of the Holy Spirit. O there is great reason to fear that another like season will never, never return upon you. O sleeper! awake, and hearken, there is a noise and a shaking among the dry bones. Some it may be of your own acquaintance, secure like you a little while ago, are now in deep concern, and can no longer relish those carnal pleasures in which you were companions. Now, destruction from God is a terror to them, and they are fleeing from the wrath to come. What a reproof doth God give to your stupidity in the awakenings of others? And here, among you with whom the Spirit is striving at this day, we behold many of our young people. O our children! God is drawing nigh to you in a distinguishing manner," &c.

Nor were the people satisfied with all these Lectures: but as private societies for religious exercises, both of younger and elder persons, both of males and females by themselves, in several parts of the town, now increased to a much greater number than ever, viz. to near the number of thirty, meeting on Lord's Day, Monday, Wednesday and Thursday evenings; so the people were constantly employing the ministers to pray and preach at

those societies, as also at many private houses,
formed society met: and such numbers flocked t
as greatly crowded them, as well as more tha_
filled our houses of public worship both on Lor
and Lectures, especially evening Lectures, for
twelvemonth after.

Some of our ministers, to oblige the peor
sometimes preached in public and private, at o,
or another, even every evening, except after Sa
for a week together: and the more we pray
preached, the more enlarged were our hearts, s
more delightful the employment. And O how
how serious and attentive were our hearers! Ho
awakened and hopefully converted by their mi
And how many of such added soon to our churc
we hope will be saved eternally? Scarce a
seemed to be preached without some good impres

As to the church to which I belong—Within 6
from the end of January, 1740–1, were threescore
to our communicants: the greater part of whom
more exact account of the work of the Spirit of
their souls in effectual calling, as described in the
minister Assembly's Shorter Catechism, than I w
to meet with before: besides many others I could
have charity for, who refrained from coming to tl
of Christ for want of a satisfying view of the
renovation in them Mr. Tennent being so ex
strict in cautioning people from running into ch
taking the sacred covenant, and receiving the Lor
per, the seal thereof, until they had saving grac
diverse brought to a very hopeful disposition, yes
I doubt not, to embrace the Savior in all his office
through fear and darkness kept from coming in
communion. Or otherwise, many more I believe
have entered; who had they the like experiences
before, I doubt not would have readily offered then
and we should have as readily received them, and
now, as some of the most hopeful Christians. So
Mr. Tennent's awakening ministry shake their ho
hinder them, that those whom I apprehended to be
and thought myself obliged to encourage, I found
pressions of his preaching had discouraged.

Yea, some who had been in full communio
made so suspicious of themselves, as to refrain pa.

I had no small pains to remove their scruples. For to my own opinion—it seems to me, that where there thirst for Christ and his spiritual benefits, that thirst raised by the Spirit of Christ: and in raising such a that, He qualifies for them, shows his readiness to satiate invites, requires, and gives sufficient grounds for coming to Him at these pipes of living waters; though we may not be sure whether this thirst arises from a renewed heart or no: and thither therefore should we come with humble sense of our emptiness and unworthiness, and with our thirsty souls reaching forth to Him, to receive from His open, offered and overflowing fulness. If I am mistaken, I desire to see it.

However, in many of these people, their convictions, in judgment of charity, appeared by the same spirit to be carried further than an awakening view of their sins, their sinfulness and misery; even to what the Assembly's Catechism, agreeable to Scripture, calls an enlightening their minds in the knowledge of Christ, or clear, lively and attractive views of His perfect suitableness, all-sufficiency and willingness as the Son of God incarnate and Mediator, to receive them, and by His merits, intercession, grace and Spirit to reconcile them to the holy God, to save and make them completely and eternally holy and happy, though now the chief of sinners: and in such views as these he melted their frozen hearts, renewed their wills, overcome them with affection to Him, and persuaded and enabled them to embrace Him in his person and all his offices and benefits as offered in the gospel.

By Dr. Colman's Letter of June 8, 1741, it appears, that in 1741, in April, there were nine or ten, and in May were nineteen, added to his church: among whom (says the Dr.) were many of the rich and polite of our sons and daughters.

And the Rev. Mr. Webb, senior Pastor of the New North, just now informs me, with respect to his church and people, in the following words—"Admissions to full communion of those hopefully wrought upon in the late day of grace, about one hundred and sixty: of which one hundred and two from January 1740–1, to 1741–2. Of those above mentioned, by far the greater part have since given hopeful signs of saving conversion. And many more give good evidences of grace; but for the reasons
   I account [above] cannot be prevailed upon to come
the Table of the Lord."

In this year, 1741, the very face of the town ~~
be strangely altered. Some who had not been ~~
the Fall before, have told me their great surpr~~
change in the general look and carriage of pe~
soon as they landed. Even the negroes and boy
streets surprisingly left their usual rudeness: I kne
of these had been greatly affected, and now were
into religious societies. And one of our worthy
men expressing his wonder at the remarkable
informed me, that whereas he used with others o
day evenings to visit the taverns, in order to cle ~~
of town inhabitants, they were wont to find man~~
and meet with trouble to get them away; but no~~
gone at those seasons again, he found them empty
but lodgers.

Of that time the Rev. Dr. Colman justly writes ~~
Rev. Dr. Watts, on September 15, 1741, in the foll
terms: "Thanks be to God in our Province the i~~
sions of religion grow and increase in a happy,~~
sedate manner, such as gives a joyous prospect ~~
to the next generation, that our young ones will b~~
grave, devout parents to their children. I know n~~
to admire the pleasant, gracious work of God. Ou
tures flourish, our Sabbaths are joyous, our Church
crease, our ministers have new life and spirit in~~
work."

Of the same time the Rev. Mr. Cooper also wri~~
Nov. 20, 1741, in his noble Preface to Mr. Edw~~
most excellent, solid, judicious and scriptural pe~~
ance, as the venerable Mr. Willison of Scotland ~~
styles it, in the following manner:—"I verily be
in this our metropolis, there were the last winter
thousands under such religious impressions as they ~~
felt before. And as to the fruits of this work, (~~
we have been bid so often to wait for) blessed be
so far as there has been time for observation, they ~~
to be abiding. I do not mean, that none have lost
impressions, or that there are no instances of hyp~~
and apostasy. Scripture and experience lead us ~~
pect these at such a season. It is to me matter o~~
prise and thankfulness, that as yet there have be~~
more. But I mean, that a great number of those
have been awakened are still seeking and striving to
in at the straight gate. The most of those who

en thought to be converted, continue to give evidences
their being new creatures, and seem to cleave to the
rd with full purpose of heart.   To be sure a new face
things continues in this town; though many circum-
nces concur to render such a work not so observable
re, as in smaller and distant places.   Many things not
coming the profession of the gospel are in a measure
formed.   Taverns, dancing-schools, and such meetings
have been called Assemblies, which have always prov-
unfriendly to serious godliness, are much less frequent-
.   Many have reduced their dress and apparel, so as to
ke them look more like the followers of the humble
sus.   And it has been both surprising and pleasant to
e how some younger people, and of that sex too which
most fond of such vanities, have put off the bravery of
eir ornaments, as the effect and indication of their seek-
g the inward glories of the King's Daughter.   Religion
now much more the subject of conversation at friends'
uses, than ever I knew it.   The doctrines of grace are
poused and relished.   Private religious meetings are
eatly multiplied.   The public assemblies (especially
ctures) are much better attended: and our auditories
re never so attentive and serious.   There is indeed
extraordinary appetite after the sincere milk of the
rd.   It is more than a twelvemonth since an evening
cture was set up in this town; there are now several;
o constantly on Tuesday and Friday evenings; when
me of our most capacious houses are well filled, with
arers, who by their looks and deportment seem to come
hear that their souls might live.   An evening in God's
urts is now esteemed better than many elsewhere.
here is also great resort to ministers in private.   Our
nds continue full of work· and many times we have
ore than we can discourse with distinctly and separ-
ely."
January 11, 1741-2, most of the associate pastors of
is town agreed on a course of Days of Prayer in their
veral churches; as the Rev. Dr. Sewall well expresses
in his sermon on that occasion, preached in the South
hurch, February 26, 1741-2, "to bless the name o
od for spiritual blessings already received in the re-
arkable revival of His work among us, and in many
her places; to seek of God the more plentiful effusion
his Holy Spirit; that the Lord would preserve us and

3

his people from every thing that hath a ten
quench his Spirit, and obstruct the progress an
of his good work; and that it may go on and pros
the whole land shall be filled with the blessed
the Spirit." And in his sermon he says, "We
praise the Lord that he has not left us without
of his divine power and grace in the wonderful open
of his Spirit in our times. Let the success which
hath of late given to the ministers of the word,
what we have known in times past, animate us to
more abundantly. And let not any pervert wha
been said, to prejudice themselves or others a
that wonderful work of grace, which I verily be
God has wrought in this town and other places."

In some, this further work of conviction and effe
calling was clearer, in others more obscure, in other
or more doubtful. And so various likewise wer
joys and consolations rising from the various chang
exercises in them, or their various applications to C
for mercy. But herein their pastors labored to pre
them from mistakes, to discover their dangers on e
side, to lead them to a thorough conviction and hu
tion, and through these to right views of Christ and
ing with him in a saving manner; that they might n
deceived with joys or consolations which belonged n
them.

Of those who came not into full communion with
churches—some who were under strong convictions,
in a hopeful way, have since sadly lost them; the S
of God has ceased striving, and they are more blind
hard than ever: and, some of these like those under H
ineffectual influence in the apostles' days; "after the
have escaped the pollution of the world, through th
knowledge of the Lord and Savior Jesus Christ, are aga
entangled therein and overcome; their latter end i
worse with them than the beginning; and it has happene
to them according to the true proverb, 'the dog is turne
to his own vomit again, and the sow that was washed t
her wallowing in the mire," 2 Peter, ii, 20—22. An
some who had fair resemblances both of saving grace an
holy joy, whereby they for a time deceived both them
selves and others; after high appearances have falle
away: as some who first followed Christ himself, yet afte
left him; and as he has represented the various even

impressions made by his own and his successors' preach-
ng, in the parable of the sower; Matt. xiii, Mark iv, and
Luke viii.

But though their faithful ministers, both in private and
public, both in preaching and print, fairly warned, and
from the word of God foretold, of these apostacies; yet
they gave occasion to the prejudiced against the work,
to cast a slur on the rest in general, to multiply and mag-
nify the instances, and pronounce them all impostors. So
I remember, when thirty years since I lived and preached in England, especially in the latter end of queen Ann's
reign; if but one of our congregation, and much more
one of our communion, fell into any scandal, all the country round would ring and echo with it, and the looser
people in the church of England would take occasion to
triumph with their reproaches; crying out, "We were
all alike, and though we were so precise we would not
curse or swear, yet we would lie, and cheat, and steal, and
commit any private wickedness;" and the profane would
damn us all as a pack of hypocrites.

And indeed in every party, where there is an enmity
or prejudice against any other person or party, there is
always more or less of blindness and partiality, and a
powerful bent, on all occasions, to misconstrue, cavil, mis-
represent, defame and vilify. So were the ancient puritans with the pious fathers of this country, treated in the
reigns of king James the I. and Charles the I. until they
came over hither between 1620 and 1640: and so were
the pious Nonconformists in the reign of king Charles the
II. I believe there scarce ever was a set of men more
reproached and stigmatized than those pious Puritans and
Nonconformists: and this not only by looser people, but
even by learned clergymen, as their writings to this day
show. And any man who knows them, may see the same
aspersing and reviling spirit and way of writing in the
present day, against the instruments and subjects of this
work in general. So the Papists have traduced the Pro-
testants in general, especially Luther, Calvin, Beza, Knox,
&c. for, by blackening those great Reformers, they thought
to blacken the Reformation advanced by them: yea, to
this very day, the most learned in the Christian world cry
out of nothing but contention and confusion in that happy
work, and deny there has been any Reformation at all;
yea, assert, that those who embraced the pretended re-

formed religion, grew insolent, censorious, turbu
worse in morals.   So I have heard an Egyptian t
who once sailed with me, most zealously repre-
Christians, from the numerous instances he kne
vilest sect on earth.   And so was their gloriou
counted a deceiver; and his apostles were despi
feted, reviled, persecuted, defamed, made as the
the world, and the offscouring of all things, 1 Co

Some, after all, have no doubt deceived both t
selves and others in the extent of their conviction
miliation, applying to Christ, and in the spring and n
of their comforts.   Some I was afraid of at the tim
not being duly convinced, humbled, broken-hearted,
condemned, devoted to God, concerned for his glor
having a due reverence of Him: and some few have
too much occasion for our fears since.   Though fro
extensive view of the many infirmities and corru
in the best of saints on earth, I am not apt to be na
or censorious in these matters: for till persons who s
ed to be converted, fall into a course of some sin or
against the common light of conscience, I am not w
to lose my charity.

But the generality of those, whom I judged to
passed through a right conviction and humiliation to
in Christ, seemed to come to consolation in Him,
way agreeable to Scripture, the very nature and re
of things, and common experience of those who
thoroughly subdued to Christ, savingly enlightened,
satisfied in Him, rest on Him, and feel themselves in
new state, happily changed and brought into the glorio
liberty of the sons of God: as I apprehend those were
and one or other of these are common springs of joy o
consolation, especially at the first conversion.

The consolations of some were weaker, of other
stronger: in some they rose to joys; in some few to jo
unspeakable and full of glory, as the apostle speaks
though I never saw one either in town or country, it
what some wrongly call a vision, trance or revelation
And where those few instances have happened in some
places, appeared but a little while and vanished.*   B

*I never heard of above one or two in this town; and I do not re
member to have heard of one in this province to the southward of u
though there has been a remarkable revival in several places in th
part of the land.

what I have heard, I apprehend that where they were unfeigned, they were only natural effects of an extraordinary intense exercise of soul; though a Divine influence might be the original of the exercise. Nor do I apprehend such effects a sign either of the person's being unsanctified or sanctified: sanctification being to be judged of by the frame of the whole soul and nature of its exercises, while fully awake, and not by such dreaming ideas: yea, though it were possible they should be inspirations, they would be no more signs in themselves of sanctification, than the genuine visions of Balaam or Belshazzar. And I know of none but is of the same opinion with me.

But as for spiritual joys and consolations; whoever has a large experience in his own heart, or a large acquaintance with the various experiences of others, has found those joys arise from such like various causes as these that follow.

1. Some in the progress of their conviction towards the depths of humiliation; while their souls were quarrelling with the holiness, justice, law, wrath, curses, truth and sovereignty of God, so as to throw them into the utmost tumult; they have been at length, and sometimes suddenly subdued, so as to yield, submit and resign into the sovereign hands of Christ: upon which their quarrels and tumults ceasing, a divine and wondrous calm and pleasure have immediately and genuinely succeeded.

2. Some from a lively view of the exceeding number and heinousness of their sins, and vileness of their hearts, whereby they thought themselves the worst of sinners; and seeing the all-sufficiency of Christ in every thing but willingness to save such horrid wretches, were in great distress; but upon seeing his willingness to save even them in particular, have been overcome with joy at the view, and with such joyful views fled into his arms.

3. Some finding themselves under the love and power of sin, in wretched bondage to their lusts, to horrible suggestions, temptations, oppositions, and utter impotence to free themselves and serve the Lord with pleasure; being unexpectedly delivered, and brought into the glorious liberty of the sons of God; they have been like those in Psalm cxxvi, "When the Lord turned again the captivity of Zion, we were like them that dream: then was our mouth filled with laughter, and our tongue with sing-

3*

ing: the Lord hath done great things for us, whereo:
are glad."

4. Some laboring under such blindness of mind,
they could see nothing of the personal and perfect lo
ness of Christ, have been exceedingly troubled; w
they came, especially on a sudden, to see his perfect
transcendant loveliness, it has raised them into a trans

5. Some who have found their hearts as hard as a r
that they could not mourn in the least, as they could
ceive, for their horrid sins and sinfulness, and were in
way of despair; upon their hearts dissolving with g
sorrow for their piercing Christ, and even the sma
sins and heart-impurities, have been greatly affected
pleasure and gladness.

6. Some after all their genuine changes, their exer
of faith in Christ, of love unto Him, repentance and ot
graces, have not yet been able to see whether these h
been any other than superficial changes and com
graces, and been in great perplexity; until the Spiri
Christ has shone so clearly on them as to give them
ful satisfaction.

7. Some having all the likely marks of conversion,
and even some of their graces in some exercise, though
very faint and low, and their hearts exceeding cold, flat
and deadened, have been greatly discouraged; but ere
they were aware, their souls have been made as the
chariots of Amminadib, to their great rejoicing.

8. Some have been so greatly troubled with their lamentable distance and estrangement from the blessed Jesus, as they could enjoy no rest; until he has taken them
into his banquetting house, exalted them to sit in heavenly
places with Him, and so shown his glories and love unto
them (his banner over them was love) as have most
powerfully drawn out their hearts to an holy and trans-
porting intimacy with Him; that in the believing views
of Christ and sensation of this communion, they have re-
joiced with joy unspeakable and full of glory. I here
write what many holy souls who have had communion
with Christ, by their experience well understand. And
by sensation, I mean in the like spiritual sense as when
Christ speaks of his supping with believers and they with
Him, Rev. iii, 20.

As for spiritual pride and rash judging—some lately
wrought upon, especially in hours of temptation, have

grievously exceeded; yea some whom we judged to be effectually called, as well as many more who had been under very powerful and far advanced, but ineffectual operations; and who ought not to be blended with, as is the way of the prejudiced, but distinguished from the other. Yet some of the hopefully renewed are more free than others from those excesses: and I never knew the most grown, humble, and prudent saint on earth wholly without them; for if I had, I should hold to sinless perfection in the present state: much less can we expect the newborn convert to be so humble and wise, as those who have been growing in grace and knowledge for several years. Alas! every soul renewed has remains of the same corruptions (though not reigning) as before; they mix with all our graces; unbelief with faith, pride with humility, precipitant zeal or passion with wisdom, rash judging of others with condemning ourselves: and he seems to be little acquainted with his own heart who sees not in himself a bent to be proud even of his own humility; and who feels not the risings of pride, especially while grace is young, even in his highest enlargements and enjoyments, as well as in his best performances and the applauses of those about him. Even the apostle Paul himself, though one of the greatest mortification and improved sanctity; yet by being favored of God with abundant revelations, found himself so strongly inclined to be above measure exalted, that if there had not been given him a thorn in the flesh, 'the messenger of Satan to buffet him,' he would have been carried away by the natural bias, 2 Cor. xii. And what wonder is it at first to see some undue elations mix with the joys of young and little experienced Christians, before they have much time to grow in the sad, surprising and abasing views of their remaining corruptions; which at the first sense of their change, their first joyful views of the love and glory of Christ, and first elevations of their faith and affections to Him, they could scarce perceive, and were therefore ready to think by His blood and Spirit to be almost entirely purged away.

But with the common mixture of their remaining infirmities and corruptions, I have generally seen attending their joys, high, humble and affectionate admirations of the wonderful grace of God, and astonishing pity and condescension of the Son of His love, in becoming incarnate, dying to save them, bearing so long with them while they have been spitting and trampling on Him; and after all their abuses, sending them His ambassadors and tenders of grace, employing His Spirit, overcoming their hearts, and opening His arms to receive them. and with these joys I have also seen all the proper expressions of their lively gratitude, love, praise, devotion to God their Savior, zeal for His glory; love to His word truths, ordinances, and those in whom the meek, humble and holy image of Christ appears, and concern for others. And as they soon found the activity of their love subsiding, the fountain of corruption in them rising, and their spiritual impotence in a sad degree returning; the Holy Spirit has given them further views of their remaining vileness; and they have generally grown more humble and jealous of themselves, more sensible of their depending on Christ continually, and more meek and tender in their carriage to others.

And thus successfully did this divine work as above described go on in town, without any lisp, as I remember, of a separation either in this town, or province, for above a year and a half after Mr. Whitefield left us, viz. the end of June, 1742; when the Rev. Mr. Davenport, of Long-Island, came to Boston. And then through the awful providence of the sovereign God, the wisdom of whose ways are past finding out, we unexpectedly came to an unhappy period, which it exceedingly grieves me now to write of, though with all convenient brevity.

Friday evening, June 25, he came to Charlestown. Lord's-day forenoon, he attended the public worship, and at the Lord's Table there: but the afternoon stayed at his lodgings, from an apprehension of the minister's being unconverted, which greatly alarmed us. Monday afternoon he came over the ferry to Boston: which the associate pastors in this town and Charlestown, then at their stated course of meeting, hearing of, sent to signify, that we should we glad to see him; whereupon he presently came, and we had long and friendly conferences with him about his conduct, on this and the following day.

On Thursday, July 1, we thought ourselves obliged to publish a declaration of our judgment concerning him: wherein we owned, "That he appeared to us to be truly pious, and we hoped that God had used him as an instrument of good to many souls; yet we judged it our duty to bear our testimony against the following particulars:—

1. His being acted much by sudden impulses. 2. His judging some ministers in Long-Island and New-England to be unconverted; and his thinking himself called of God to demand of his brethren, from place to place, an account of their regenerate state, when or in what manner the Holy Spirit wrought upon and renewed them. 3. His going with his friends singing through the streets and highways, to and from the houses of worship on Lord's days and other days. 4. His encouraging private brethren (i. e. who are not probationers for the ministry) to pray and exhort (i. e. like ministers) in assemblies gathered for that purpose. We judged it therefore our present duty not to invite him into our places of public worship, as otherwise we might have readily done." And we concluded thus—"And we take this opportunity to repeat our testimony to the great and glorious work of God, which of His free grace he has begun and is carrying on in many parts of this and the neighboring provinces; beseeching him to preserve, defend, maintain and propagate it, in spite of all the devices of Satan against it, of one kind or other; that however it may suffer by the imprudence of its friends, or by the virulent opposition of its enemies, yet it may stand as on the rock, and the gates of hell may never prevail against it."

Boston, July 1, 1742.

THOMAS FOXCROFT, *Pastor of the First Church.*
JOSHUA GEE, *Pastor of the Second, or Old North.*
JOSEPH SEWALL, } *Pastors of the Old South.*
THOMAS PRINCE, }
WILLIAM COOPER, } *Pastors of the Church in*
BENJAMIN COLMAN, } *Brattle-street.*
JOHN WEBB, } *Pastors of the New North.*
ANDREW ELIOT, }
SAMUEL CHECKLEY, *Pastor of the New South.*
WILLIAM WELSTEED } *Pastors of the New Brick*
ELLIS GRAY, } *Church.*
MATHER BYLES, *Pastor of the Church in Hollis-street.*
HULL ABBOT, *Pastor of the Church at Charlestown.*
THOMAS PRENTICE, *do. do.*

Upon publishing this declaration on Friday, many were offended: and some days after, Mr. Davenport thought himself obliged to begin in his public exercises to declare against us also; naming some as unconverted, represent ing the rest as Jehosaphat in Ahab's army, and exhort ti the people to separate from us: which so diverted t minds of many from being concerned about their o conversion, to think and dispute about the case of oth as not only seemed to put an awful stop to their awak ings, but also on all sides to inflame our passions, and pro voke the Holy Spirit in a gradual and dreadful measure t withdraw His influence.

Now a disputatious spirit most grievously prevail among us: and, what almost ever attends it, much ce soriousness and reflection; which had a further tendency to inflame and alienate, and whereof many of every part were sadly guilty. It was indeed a lamentable time wherein we seemed to fall into such a case as the Chri tian church at Corinth, in the Apostle's days: which had shared such a large effusion of the Holy Spirit, that the Apostle calls them "sanctified in Christ; and thanked his God always in their behalf for the grace of God which was given them by Jesus Christ, that in every thing they were enriched by him in all utterance and all knowledge even as the testimony of Christ was confirmed in them so that they came behind in no gift:" and yet he com plains there were risen among them "contentions, envy ing, strife, divisions; one saying, I am of Paul, another, I am of Apollos"—and they were "carnal, and walked as men," &c 1 Cor i, and iii.

And now a small number from some of our Churches and Congregations* (some had been communicants for merly, and some added lately) withdrew, and met in a dis tinct society: whereof four males, and two or three fe males, were of our communion.

In the following month came out of the press in Boston, a book composed by the Rev. Mr. Dickinson of Elizabeth Town, New-Jersey, entitled, "A display of God's special grace: in a familiar dialogue between a minister and a gentleman of his congregation, about the work of God, in the conviction and conversion of sinners, so remarka bly of late begun and going on in these American parts. Wherein the objections against some uncommon appear ances among us are distinctly considered, mistakes recti-

* There were ten Congregational Churches in town, two Presby terian, one Baptist, and three Episcopalian.

fied, and the work itself particularly proved to be from the Holy Spirit. With an addition, in a second conference, relating to sundry Antinomian principles, beginning to obtain in some places. To which is prefixed, an attestation, by several ministers of Boston."

And the principal paragraphs of the Attestation are as follows:—"He must be a stranger in Israel, who has not heard of the uncommon religious appearances in the several parts of this land, among persons of all ages and characters. This is an affair which has in some degree drawn every one's attention, and been the subject of much debate both in conversation and writing. And the grand question is, 'Whether it be a work of God, and how far it is so?' The most serious and judicious, both ministers and Christians, have looked upon it to be, in the main, a genuine work of God, and the effect of that effusion of the Spirit of grace, which the faithful have been praying, hoping, longing and waiting for; while at the same time they have looked upon some circumstances attending it, to be from natural temper, human weakness, or the subtilty and malice of Satan, permitted to counteract this divine operation. But here rightly to distinguish is a matter of no small difficulty; and requires both a scriptural knowledge of, and an experimental acquaintance with the things of the Spirit of God. Mr. Edwards's Discourse concerning the distinguishing marks of a work of the Spirit of God, has met with deserved acceptance, and been of great use. The following performance, by another dear and reverend brother in a different part of the country, is also, in our opinion, exceeding well adapted to serve the same design, viz. to help people to judge of the present work, whether, and how far it is of God; and to remove those prejudices, which may keep them from owning it to the honour of God. and from coming under the power of it to their own salvation. Here the reader will see the ordinary work of the Spirit of grace, in applying the redemption purchased by Christ to particular souls, judiciously described, in several distinct parts of it, conviction, conversion, and consolation: the necessity of regeneration and faith, in order to final salvation, and the necessity of conviction and humiliation in order to these, clearly evinced, from the reason and nature of the thing, as well as the method God has established in His word: mistakes, which might prove fatal and undoing, carefully guarded against: and very safe suitable directions given to one who is awakened to the inquiry, 'What must I do to be saved?'. Whoever takes up this book and reads, has, as it were, in his hand glass, in which he may behold what manner of person is; whether a natural or renewed man, a hypocrite or sound believer. And in recommending this book to the world, we would be understood as owning, and bearing public testimony to, what is called the present work of God in this land, as it is here stated and distinguished (separate from those disorders, errors, and delusions which are only the unhappy accidents sometimes accompanying of it) to be such a glorious display of the Divine power and grace, as may well raise our wonder, excite our praises, and engage our prayers for the preservation and progress of it. May the children of God then unite in that prayer, Let thy work appear more and more unto thy servants, and thy glory unto their children; and the beauty of the Lord our God be upon us!"

> BENJAMIN COLMAN,
> JOSEPH SEWALL,
> THOMAS PRINCE,
> JOHN WEBB,
> WILLIAM COOPER,
> THOMAS FOXCROFT,
> JOSHUA GEE.

Boston, August 10, 1742.

In December was printed here, a treatise of the Rev. Mr. Gilbert Tennent against the Moravian errors: which treatise was introduced with a preface by several ministers of this town, and the final paragraph thereof is this:—

"When this our dear brother, whose praise is in our churches through the provinces, visited us at Boston two years ago, and in the spirit of the Rev. Mr. Whitefield entered into his labors here; it pleased God in a wonderful manner to crown his abundant services with success in the conviction and (we trust) conversion of many souls. As therefore the name of Mr. Tennent is greatly endeared to us, so we beseech our ascended Savior, the Head of the Church, long to continue him for a burning light and extensive blessing to our provinces; and in particular

use this faithful, judicious and seasonable endeavor of
his servant, for a guard and defence about his own sacred
truths and his glorious work in the midst of us, which too
many are ready to speak evil of and oppose.

BENJAMIN COLMAN,
THOMAS PRINCE,
JOHN WEBB,
WILLIAM COOPER,
THOMAS FOXCROFT,
JOSHUA GEE.

Boston, December 22, 1742.

Some time after, a man of the separate society became
a Saturday-Baptist: who being immersed in the country,
and having hands laid on him, thought himself a minister,
drew five women after him and proceeded to immerse
them: yet they all have since deserted him. But six males
of the said society, with one of Brookline, a town about
five miles off, went on to associate as a church, owning the
Assembly's Confession of Faith, and professing themselves
Congregational, according to our New-England Platform:
and have not yet returned to the several churches whence
they went; though the Rev. Mr. Davenport has happily
seen and most ingenuously confessed his abovesaid
errors and misconduct, and published his retractations.
See Christian History, No. 82, and 83.

Besides the aforesaid four males and two or three
females of the South Church, I know not any who have
left our communion. But the rest of our said numerous
and former additions continue with us; and as far as I
know, their conversation is as becomes the gospel.* Nor
do I hear of more than one of those who have left our
church that has fallen into other censurable evil, nor in
the other churches in town, except a few of the New
North.

July 7, 1743, there met in Boston one of the largest
assembly of ministers that ever convened here, to bear
their testimony to this remarkable revival in the land:
when ten ministers of this town, joined with many others
in giving their public testimony to this happy work. An

* This the reader will recollect was written in November, 1744,
more than four years after the revival.

4

account of which is printed in the Christian History, 20, &c.

On December 13, following, this town and land ceived a great loss in the death of the Rev. Mr. Coo. An account of which, with his deserved character, No. 43, of the Christian History. To which I would the further account of the Rev. Dr. Colman in his Funer Sermon the Lord's day after, since published, in the lowing terms:—

"Mr. Cooper was as fixed and firm against the spirit of separation from the churches of New-England, whic he judged to be strongly settled on the platform of Scrip ture; as any rock on our coast is unshaken by the furiea waves that only break themselves into foam by dashing against it. And had he lived he would have been a most strenuous opposer of this defection. But at the same time he was immoveably determined, as we all know that there has been a remarkable work of God going among us, by what he had seen with his eyes, had looke upon, and as it were handled, in the resort to him (at some other ministers of the town) of a multitude of per sons, younger and older, under strong convictions, humi iation, illuminations, godly fear, with strong crying an tears; faith, hope, trust, joy, with strong reliance on th righteousness of Christ for justification, and on the Al mighty Spirit of grace in a sovereign manner to enabl them unto all the duties of a sober, righteous and godl life; to work in them both to will and to do, to begin an carry on His good work in their souls; and to keep then by His mighty power through faith to salvation. An among these there were numbers overflowing with th joys and comforts of religion, in the utmost abhorrence o themselves, and repenting as in dust and ashes; while th love of God seemed to be shed abroad in their hearts, i their fervent desires after and pleasure in the convictio and conversion of others. The numerous instances o this nature, with whom he daily conversed, gave hin abundant satisfaction of the presence and power of th Sanctifier and Comforter in and with many of them. think myself also now called by the providence of Go to add,—that as I was myself struck with wonder at wha of this nature occurred to me two years ago among th young people of this flock, so the good fruits of thei abiding profession unto this day, in a discreet, meek, vir

tuous, pious conversation, gave me satisfaction and pleasure in them from day to day; while their exemplary
face of grave devotion, and diligent attention to the word
of God, on Lord's-days and Lectures, are also adorning to
the doctrine of God their Savior."

Of all who resorted to me from all the Congregations
in town, I remember no more than three or four who
talked of their impulses: and but one or two of these a
subject of the late revival, the other two had been
communicants in two of our churches, and used to speak
of those things before. Nor in all the preaching of the
instruments of this work in town, did I ever hear any
teach to follow impulses, or any religious impressions,
but of the word of God upon our minds, affections, wills
and consciences; and which, agreeable to the Holy Scripture, the most famous Reformers and Puritan ministers
both in England, Scotland, and New-England, have in
their writings taught us.

As to the doctrinal principles of those who continue in
our Congregations, and have been the subjects of the late
revival; they are the same as they have been all along
instructed in, from the Westminister Assembly's Shorter
Catechism: which has been generally received and
taught in the churches of New-England from its first
publication for these hundred years to this day; and
which is therefore the system of doctrine most generally
and clearly declarative of the faith of the New-England
churches.

And though some have represented many of the subjects of this work as holding some or other of the following mischievous errors; viz. 1. "That sanctifying grace
in a minister is necessary to render the administrations of
gospel ordinances valid. 2. That unconverted ministers
are incapable to be instruments of converting people.
3. That sanctification (as described in the Assembly's
Shorter Catechism) is no evidence of justification. 4.
That an unregenerate man ought not to pray. And 5,
That assurance is essential to saving faith, so as whoever
believes, is sure he believes in a saving manner, and is
not in doubt or darkness about it." Upon a careful inquiry, I cannot find nor hear of any of the subjects of this
work remaining in our several congregations in town; no,
nor even in that which has drawn off from us, who hold
these or any other familistical or Antinomian errors.

However, the sovereign Spirit in his awakening
ence in the unconverted, and his enlivening effic₁
the hopefully renewed, in this town, has seemed
two last years in a gradual and awful manner to with
For a twelvemonth I have rarely heard the cry ₁
new ones—"What shall I do to be saved?" But fe
now added to our churches, and the heavenly show
Boston seems to be over. Of those who were in th
effusion wrought on, divers are sometimes repairi
me, with sad complaints of their spiritual dulness,
ness and decays; but I hope are working out their
tion with fear and trembling: while some have no'
then a fresh revival of grace and comfort.

Thus have I endeavored a brief and plain accou
the late Revival in this town; especially among th₁
ple who resorted to me, and more particularly those
the Assembly I belong to, according to my observati
and intelligence: relating only those facts which seem
to me, as I went along, to be most material; avoiding p₁
sonal reflections, and writing, as I always desire, w₁
candor and moderation. I leave it as a grateful pub
testimony of the memorable work of the Divine Pow
and grace among us in my day, which my eyes have se₁
and my ears have heard with pleasure; that God ₁
Father, Son and Spirit, may have the more extend₁
praise, to whose blessing I consign it; and that oth₁
may thereby receive eternal benefit.

THOMAS PRINCE.

Boston, November 26, 1744.

have given the Public some account of the late
:raordinary work of God in this metropolis of New-
gland; we think it convenient to insert some ac-
ints of the Rev. GEORGE WHITEFIELD, an eminent in-
ument thereof, as they successively arrived, before
appearance here, and which prepared the way
his entertainment and successful labors among us.

was in the year 1738, we were first surprised with
ews of Mr. Whitefield, as a young minister of the
ch of England, of flaming piety and zeal for the
r of godliness: who this year sailed from London to
iltar and Georgia; being appointed minister of Fred-
in that Province, and after a few months stay, re-
d, through Ireland, to England, for priest's orders,
· ordained only a deacon before.
ie year following, we were yet more surprised to
of his preaching the doctrines of the martyrs and
· Reformers, which were the same our forefathers
ght over hither: particularly the great doctrines of
ial sin, of regeneration by the Divine Spirit, justifi-
ı by faith only, &c. and this with amazing assiduity,
r and success: which extraordinary appearance,
:ially in the church of England, together with the
nultitudes of people that flocked to hear him, drew
ttention to every thing that was published concern-
im.
ie latter end of this year he left England, being pre-
d by the honorable Trustees of Georgia to the
ç at Savannah: and arrived at Philadelphia the second
ovember, preached there on Lord's day, and every
n the week after. November 8th, began to preach
the Court House gallery about six a night, to near
iousand people, who stood in awful silence to hear
and so every night, until Lord's day evening. No-

4*

vember 12th, he set out for New York: where he arri
two days after, and there also preached with great po
and efficacy. An account of which, with some more
ticular description of his person and doctrines, were d
up by an ingenious gentleman, and published in the M
England Journal, from which we select the follow
passages:—

"The Rev. Mr. Whitefield arrived at the city of N
York on Wednesday, the 14th inst. a little before n
The next day in the afternoon, he preached in the f
to many hundreds of people.

"Among the hearers, the person who gives this acco
was one. I fear curiosity was the motive that led
and many others into that assembly. I had read two
three of Mr. Whitefield's sermons, and part of his Jou
and from thence had obtained a settled opinion, that
was a good man. Thus far was I prejudiced in his fa
But then having heard of much opposition, and m
clamors against him, I thought it possible that he m
have carried matters too far. That some enthus
might have mixed itself with his piety, and that his
might have exceeded his knowledge. With these
possessions I went into the fields; when I came the
saw a great number of people, consisting of Christia
all denominations, some Jews, and a few, I believe,
had no religion at all. When Mr. Whitefield came t
place before designed; which was a little eminence o
side of a hill; he stood still and beckoned with his h
and disposed the multitude upon the descent, before,
on each side of him. He then prayed most excelle
in the same manner that the first ministers of the Ch
tian Church prayed (before they were shackled
forms.) The assembly soon appeared to be divided
two companies, the one of which I considered under
name of God's church, and the other the devil's cha
The first were collected round the minister, and w
very serious and attentive. The last had placed the
selves in the skirts of the assembly, and spent most
their time in giggling, scoffing, talking and laughing.
believe the minister saw them, for in his sermon, obs
ing the cowardice and shamefacedness of Christian
Christ's cause, he pointed towards this assembly,
reproached the former with the boldness and zeal
which the devil's vassals serve him. Towards the

prayer, the whole assembly appeared more united, and all became hushed and still; a solemn awe and reverence appeared in the faces of most, a mighty energy attended the word. I heard and felt something astonishing and surprising, but, I confess, I was not at that time fully rid of my scruples. But as I thought I saw a visible presence of God with Mr. Whitefield, I kept my doubts to myself.

"Under this frame of mind, I went to hear him in the evening at the Presbyterian church, where he expounded to above two thousand people within and without doors. I never in my life saw so attentive an audience: Mr. Whitefield spake as one having authority: all he said was demonstration, life and power! The people's eyes and ears hung on his lips. They greedily devoured every word. I came home astonished! every scruple vanished; I never saw nor heard the like; and I said within myself, Surely God is with this man of a truth. He preached and expounded in this manner twice every day, for four days, and his evening assemblies were continually increasing.

"On Sunday morning, at eight o'clock, his congregation consisted of about fifteen hundred people But at night, several thousands came together to hear him; and the place being too strait for them, many were forced to go away, and some (it is said) with tears lamented their disappointment. After sermon, he left New York, at ten at night, to fulfil a promise that he had made to preach at Elizabethtown, at 11 A. M. the next day.

"Mr. Whitefield was born at Gloucester, it is said, in the month of December, 1714. He observes in his Journal, that he was baptized at the font of one of the churches in that city, on the 25th day of that month. He was bred up in the bosom of the church of England, and educated at Oxford. There he commenced Batchelor of Arts. He was ordained priest, according to the orders of the church of England, on the 14th of January last, which was almost as soon as it could be, by the canons of the church, he being then but little more than twenty-four years old. He is a man of a middle stature, of a slender body, of a fair complexion, and of a comely appearance. He is of a sprightly, cheerful temper, acts and moves with great agility and life. The endowments of his mind are very uncommon; his wit is quick and piercing; his imagination lively and florid; and, as far as I can discern, both are under the direction of an exact and solid judgment. He has a most ready memory, and, I think, speaks entirely without notes. He has a clear and musical voice, and a wonderful command of it. He uses much gesture, but with great propriety: every accent of his voice, every motion of his body, speaks, and both are natural and unaffected. If his delivery is the product of art, it is certainly the perfection of it, for it is entirely concealed. He has a great mastery of words, but studies much plainness of speech.

His doctrine is right sterling, I mean, perfectly agreeable to the articles of the church of England, to which he frequently appeals for the truth of it. He loudly proclaims all men by nature to be under sin, and obnoxious to the wrath and curse of God. He maintains the absolute necessity of supernatural grace, to bring men out of this state. He asserts the righteousness of Christ to be the alone cause of the justification of a sinner; that this is received by faith; that this faith is the gift of God; that where faith is wrought, it brings the sinner under the deepest sense of his guilt and unworthiness to the footstool of sovereign grace, to accept of mercy, as the free gift of God, only for Christ's sake. He denies that good works have any share in our justification; that indeed they do justify our faith, and necessarily flow from it, as streams from the fountain; but Christ's external righteousness imputed to us, and his inherent righteousness wrought in us, is the only cause of man's salvation. He asserts the absolute necessity of the new-birth; where a principle of new life is ingenerated in the heart of man, and an entire change is produced in the temper and disposition of the soul: that this new production is solely the work of God's blessed Spirit. That wherever it is wrought, it is a permanent and abiding principle, and that the gates of hell shall never prevail against it. He asserts, that the special influence and indwelling of the Spirit, was not peculiar to the first Christians, but that it is the common privilege of believers, in all ages of the Church. That the Holy Spirit is the Author of the sanctification and comfort of all God's people. And that even in these days, if any man hath not the Spirit of Christ, he is none of His. That to many of his hearers, he feared he spake in an unknown tongue. He acknowledged that he preached great mysteries, but true Christians knew wha he meant, and that all his hearers must be brougl

understand them if ever they are saved. These are
some of those doctrines that have been attended with
such mighty power in this city! This is the doctrine of
the Church of England! This is the faith of its martyrs!
This they sealed with their blood! Notwithstanding that
so many in our days have departed from it.

He speaks much the language of the New Testament;
and has an admirable faculty in explaining the Scriptures.
He strikes out of them such lights, and unveils those ex-
cellencies which surprise his hearers, when he expounds
them. He expresses the highest love and concern for
the souls of men; and speaks of Christ with the most
affectionate appropriation—'My Master!' 'My Lord!' He
is no enemy to the innocent freedoms and liberties of
the gospel. Nor affects singularity in indifferent things.
He spends not his zeal in trifles: he says, the kingdom of
God consists not in meats and drinks, but in righteousness
and peace, and joy in the Holy Ghost. He breathes a
most catholic spirit! He prays most earnestly, that God
would destroy all that bigotry and party zeal, that has
divided Christians. He supposes that some of Christ's
flock are to be found under every denomination. He
upbraids the uncharitableness of those, that confine the
Church to their own Communion. He professes a most
sincere love to all them that love our Lord Jesus Christ
in sincerity. He declares that he has no design to make
a party in religion. That his whole view in preaching
the gospel, is to bring men to Christ, to deliver them
from their false confidences, to raise them from their dead
formalities, to revive primitive Christianity among them;
and if he can obtain this end, he will leave them to their
liberty, and they may go to what church, and worship
God in what form they like best."

This account of Mr. Whitefield excited an earnest desire in many pious people among us, to see and hear him.
But we were informed soon after, of his having preached
eight times at New York, and at several places in his
eturn to Philadelphia, of his arriving there, November
23, preaching twice every day in the church, to crowded
assemblies of people: and that, at his farewell sermon,
November 28, a multitude, computed at not less than
ten thousand, attended in the fields; that next day he left
the city, to pass through Maryland, Virginia, North and
South Carolina, to Georgia.

After this we had a brief account of his* travelling preaching through those countries, and beginning Orphan House at Savannah in Georgia.

In April, 1740, we had an account of his arrival a at Philadelphia, of his preaching there and in the ne boring places, when the congregations were greatly fected, of his setting out for New York, and his inten to return from thence to Philadelphia, and thenc Georgia, before he came to Boston; where he desig God willing, to be in July or August.

* The following historical passage, relating to the occasion, & his itinerancy, extracted from a Letter of his to the Rev. Mr. Chu prebendary of St. Paul's, London, we think proper to insert here "I wish every non-resident minister in England could give as an account of their non-residence, as I of my absence from Savai To satisfy you, Rev. Sir, I will acquaint you with the whole. WI first went abroad, I was appointed to be minister of Frederica upon my arrival in Georgia, finding there was no minister at Savai and no place of worship at Frederica, by the advice of magistrate people I continued at Savannah, teaching publicly, and from hou house, and catechising the children day by day, during the whole of my continuance at Georgia; except about a fortnight, in wh went to Frederica, to visit the people, and to see about building church, for which I had given fifty pounds out of some money I had collected, and of which I have given the public an account In about four months, I came over to England, to receive priest's orders, and collect money for building an Orphan-House. At the request of many, the honorable Trustees presented me to the living of Savannah. I ac cepted it, but refused the stipend of fifty pounds per annum, which they generously offered me. Neither did I put them to any expense during my stay in England; where I thought it my duty to abide until I had collected a sufficient sum wherewith to begin an Orphan House, though I should have left England sooner, had I not been prevented by the embargo. However I was more easy, because the honorable Trustees, I knew, had sent over another minister soon after I left the col my Upon my second arrival at Georgia, finding the case of the Orphan House, and the case of the parish, too great a task for me, I immediately wrote over to the honorable Trustees to provide another minister

In the mean while, as most of my parishioners were in debt, or ready to leave the colony, for want of being employed, and as I be lieved erecting an Orphan House would be the best thing I could do for them and their posterity, I thought it my duty from time to time to answer the invitations that were sent me to preach Christ Jesus in several parts of America, and to raise farther collections towards car rying on the Orphan House The Lord stirred up many to be ready to distribute, and willing to communicate on this occasion. I always came home furnished with provisions and money, most of which was expended among the people, and by this means the northern part of the colony almost entirely subsisted for a considerable time. This was asserted not very long ago before the honorable House of Commons. And now, Sir, judge you, whether my non-residence was any thing like the non-residence of most of the English clergy. When I was absent from my parishioners, I was not loitering or living at ease, but preaching Christ Jesus, and begging for them and theirs, &c."

An account of the fruits of his fervent ministry in these places, we had in a Letter of his to a friend in England, dated at the city of New Brunswick, in New Jersey: as follows:—

"A fortnight ago, after a short passage of ten days, I landed at Pennsylvania, and have had the pleasure of seeing and hearing that my poor endeavors for promoting Christ's kingdom, when here last, were not in vain in the Lord. I cannot well tell you how many come to me laboring under the deepest convictions, and seemingly truly desirous of finding rest in Jesus Christ, several have received Him into their hearts by faith, and have not only righteousness and peace, but also joy in the Holy Ghost.

"In short, the word has run and been glorified. I daily receive fresh and most importunate invitations to preach in all the countries round about," &c.

Some weeks before his arrival here, came out a sermon of the Rev. Mr. Smith, of Charleston, South Carolina, on the character and preaching of Mr. Whitefield there, with a Preface, by the Rev. Dr. Colman and Mr. Cooper of Boston; from which we shall extract some passages.

"The following Discourse was inclosed to us by our dear brother, the worthy author of it; and we have read it with high pleasure and satisfaction. The design is sufficiently intimated in the title-page. It is indeed a sermon of an extraordinary nature. To give, from the pulpit, the personal and ministerial character of a living preacher, is very unusual, or, perhaps, altogether new. But so is the occasion—and the Discourse must be looked upon to be apological, rather than encomiastic. The manifest design is to support the cause by vindicating the man; not a private and party cause, but that of primitive piety and catholic Christianity; the cause of Christ and truth, if the peculiar doctrines of the gospel, the asserting and clearing whereof was the glory of the Reformation, may be so called: a cause this in which zeal is certainly a virtue!

"As to the Rev. Mr. Whitefield, the person referred to and named, he is the wonder of the age; and no one man more employs the pens, and fills up the conversation of people, than he does at this day: none more admired and applauded by some, contemned and reproached by others: the *common lot of the most excellent men the world has ever had to show!*

"While so many others are speaking and publishing their sentiments concerning him with all freedom, Mr. Smith thought himself not precluded. He has had as much opportunity as most, to inform himself concerning Mr. Whitefield's doctrine, manner of life, purpose, faith, charity, long-suffering, patience, persecutions, and afflictions, which have come unto him: and what he has seen and heard, that declares he unto us; and we receive his testimony, because we know him to be a gentleman of good sense, and strict veracity; and also free from enthusiastic impressions, unless serious religion and experimental piety are so called, as we have melancholy occasion to observe they often are. There appear to us plain marks of sincerity and impartiality in the following account. And the same things have been reported to us by other Reverend Brethren, of the like character, whom we know and correspond with, in places which Mr. Whitefield has visited and preached in.

"And as to his thoughts respecting the views of Providence, in raising up men of this stamp and spirit in our day, he expresses them with great modesty and caution, and we cannot but apprehend they are countenanced from Scripture, reason, and observation.

"When God is about to carry on salvation work with any remarkable success, He will raise up suitable instruments to work by. He will form and spirit men for great and extraordinary undertakings, when He has any great and extraordinary purposes to serve.

"Thus when God's time for that great and good work of building the second temple was come, Joshua and others were animated to undertake it; and though they were men wondered at, for the warmth of their zeal, and the boldness of their enterprise; that in the face of so many opposers and difficulties, they should undertake to rebuild the holy city and the temple; yet they were raised above all discouragements, and stood firm against all opposition, being fortified with a special promise of the Messiah, in whose strength, and by whose influence they should be successfully carried on in their work 'Hear now, O Joshua, the high priest, thou and thy lows that sit before thee; for they are men wondere for I will bring forth my Servant, the Branch. Bel the Stone that I have laid before Joshua: upon one s shall be seven eyes. I will engrave the engra ereof, saith the Lord of Hosts; and I will remove the iquity of that land in one day.' Zech. iii, 8, 9.

"So when the gospel church was to be set up in the world, and the Gentile nations to be converted to the nowledge and faith of Jesus, a dozen poor illiterate shermen, were endued with power from on high, and ent forth to open men's eyes, to turn them from darkness to light, and from the power of satan unto God. And n them was fulfilled that which is written, 'Out of the mouth of babes and sucklings hast thou ordained strength, because of thine enemies; that thou mightest still the enemy and the avenger.' Psalm viii, 2.

"And when the Church was overspread with Popish darkness, superstition and idolatry, and the Romish tyranny was at its very height,* it pleased God to enlighten some ecclesiastics gradually in the knowledge of His truth, and then animate and assist them to lay open the errors and corruptions of Popery, and boldly to assert and maintain the pure truths of the gospel. Of this number were Zuinglius in Switzerland, and Luther in Germany: names that will be had in everlasting remembrance in the records of the Church.

"The resolute opposition that was made against them, and the contempt that was poured upon them, instead of cooling, inflamed their courage. The further search they made into the depth of those corruptions that had overspread the Church, the more light still broke in upon them. They found its doctrines poisoned with heresy, and its worship corrupted with superstition and idolatry; and Christianity grown very like to Paganism. Under this conviction they loudly called upon all that had any concern for their souls, to go out of Babylon, as they would not be partakers of her plagues. And multitudes of people were influenced by their preaching and writing, to renounce the Roman doctrines and superstitions; and many of the princes of Europe too, were inclined to favor and fall in with the Reformation.

"As for Luther in particular, he was a wondrous man, and the almighty power of God was eminently manifested in him. When he first appeared, 'What could be expected from a poor friar, creeping out of a cloister?' He was advised by his friends to get into his cell again, and

* In the 16th century.

to ply his prayers, and not venture upon so hazardou
undertaking as to preach against the Pope, or attemp
impossible a work as the Reformation.' But, no
might, nor power, out by my Spirit, saith the Lor
Hosts. This single inconsiderable man was more th
match for the powers of Rome, and was instrument:
produce one of the greatest changes the world has
had to marvel at.

"And when it pleases God to renew the face of reli;
when primitive Christianity, and the power of godli'
shall be revived in the reforming churches; when
professors of the gospel shall be recovered from
false principles they have embraced, raised above t
dead formalities they have so long rested in, and awo
ed out of that lethargy they are fallen into; when t
expected times of reformation shall come on, is if
reasonable to suppose God will raise up those to effe
whom he will furnish with a good measure of the p
tive apostolic spirit; whose hearts shall be inflamed
a burning zeal for the honor of the Redeemer, and
to the souls of men; and who shall therefore be wins
to deny themselves in those things which are dear to th
most; shall not scruple to go out of the common road,
spread the triumphs of the gospel, and fetch in souls
Jesus Christ; and will not be discouraged by any oppo
tion they may meet with? Considering the present stat
of things in the Christian world, how can we expect an
great change for the better, but in a way that shall
extraordinary?

"And if there is any appearance of such a work at an
time, or in any places, surely we should take care not t
slight and undervalue it; much less should we reproac
and censure it, or those who are used as instruments in
but, on the contrary, we should rejoice in it, so far as i
seems to be from heaven, and further it with our pray
ers, as those who are waiting for the kingdom of God.

"We would therefore bespeak the prayers of th
faithful in Christ Jesus, into whose hands these paper
may come, both for our dear brother, the author of
this Discourse, who is with great zeal contending fo
some important points of the faith once delivered to th
saints, against some who openly oppose them, and labo
ing to promote practical godliness, in the place wher
divine Providence has appointed his present station; tha

he may be assisted and succeeded in all his faithful services for the Redeemer's kingdom: and also for the Rev.
Mr. Whitefield, that he may (as he has well expressed himself in some of his Letters to us) 'be kept humble and
dependent on our dear Lord Jesus;' be preserved in his
travels, strengthened to his uncommon labors, and fortified
against all opposition: that satan (who cannot but have a
peculiar enmity at those who so set themselves against
his kingdom) may never get advantage of him, to the
blemish or hindrance of the great and good work which
we hope is begun and going on: that God would cause
him always to triumph in Christ, while he makes manifest the savor of His knowledge by him in every place,
and uses him as an instrument to bring back many wan-
dering sheep to the Shepherd and Bishop of their souls:
and very particularly that his purposed coming to us, may
be with as full a blessing of the gospel of Christ as other
places have experienced, and much more abundant, by
the will and grace of our God!

BENJAMIN COLMAN,
WILLIAM COOPER.

Boston, N. E. June 7, 1740.

*Extracts from Mr. Smith's Sermon on the Character, &c.
of Mr. Whitefield.*

Others have freely spoken their sentiments, and I have
heard the defaming, as well as the applause of many; I
said, therefore, I will answer also for my part; I also will
shew my opinion.

1. I shall give you my opinion of the doctrines he insisted on among us. To speak more generally, they
were doctrines, I am of opinion, agreeable to the dictates
of reason, evidently founded upon Scripture, exactly cor-
respondent with the articles of the establishment, of great
use and necessity in forming the Christian life; which I
had early imbibed from the best writers and systems.

To be particular,   •

One of the doctrines, which he has hardly passed over
in silence in any single Discourse, is that of original sin.
By which, I mean nothing less than the imputation of
Adam's first sin to all his posterity by ordinary generation;
which imputation is the resultance of his being constituted
to act for them in the extensive character of a legal re-

presentative; the consequence of which is that inher
corruption of nature and those sinful propensions we
now born with into the world.

Another doctrine, we have lately had in the warm
language impressed upon us, is that Pauline one of ju
fication by faith alone. And here you will remem
how the preacher vindicated himself from all suspic
of Antinomian error: for while he earnestly conten
for our justification as the free gift of God, by faith al
in the blood of Christ, he took special care to gu
against the abuse of it, and asserted that good works w
the necessary fruits and evidences of true faith.

Regeneration was another great doctrine insisted
hardly a single sermon but he mentioned it, someti
more than twice; and one, and perhaps the best of
discourses, was *ex professo* on this subject.

Another doctrine nearly allied to this, was warmly
sisted on, viz. the impressions, or, which was the prea
er's own phrase, inward feelings of the Spirit. And h
you remember, how he guarded against the invidi
censure of assuming the character of an apostle.
renounced all pretensions to the extraordinary pow
and signs of apostleship. He also allowed these feelin
of the Spirit were not in every person, or at all times,
the same degree, and that though a full assurance we
attainable, yet not of absolute necessity to the being o
Christian. Only he asserted that we might feel the Sp
of God in his sanctifying and saving impressions and w
nessing with our spirits. And what is there in this
what is agreeable to reason? How can we be led by
Spirit, or have joy in the Holy Ghost, without some s
sible perception of it? Can I at any time feel my soul
sacred raptures, burning with the love of God and Chr
and all my best passions alive: can I feel a secret pl
sure in the word, ordinances and communion with G
can I taste the powers of the world to come: can I
the threatenings of God impressed upon my consci
or promises of paradise working upon my hopes:
groan under the burthen of my corruptions, or ex
the liberty of spirit I may have, in a calm and r
hour, in the meditation of my pardon, and of heave
immortality. And yet this doctrine of feeling the
be ridiculed in an age of infidelity. This is a docti
have been acquainted with these many years. You

eard me preach it scores of times, though perhaps
clothed in other expressions. And however derided by
some, I hope always to have enthusiasm enough to maintain that the Spirit of God may be felt.

To conclude, all the doctrines now mentioned are
primitive, Protestant, Puritanic ones; which our good
forefathers, Conformists, and Dissenters, filled their writings with; and, as Dr. Watts has well observed, they filled
heaven apace, for God was with them."

Yet all that reverence, with which I heard these doctrines, from the mouth of our preacher, could not win
my approbation of some few harsher expressions which
dropt from his lips. These in my opinion may be pro-
nounced failings; but such as often attend a warm zeal
for Orthodoxy in matters of the last importance, and are
found interwoven with the brightest characters.

I shall next give you my opinion of the manner of his
preaching.

He appeared to me, in all discourses, very deeply affected and impressed in his own heart. How did that
burn within him, when he spake of the things touching
the king! With what a flow of words did he speak to us
upon the great concern of our souls! In what a flaming
light did he set out eternity before us! How earnestly
did he press Christ upon us! How close, strong and
pungent, were his applications to the conscience; ming-
ling light and heat, pointing the arrows of the Almighty
at the heart of sinners, while he poured in the balm on
the wounds of the contrite! How bold and courageous
did he look! He was no flatterer: he taught the way of
God in truth, and regarded not the persons of men; the
politest, and the most modish of our vices, he struck at;
the most fashionable entertainments; regardless of every
one's presence, but His in whose name he spake.

I shall now show my opinion of his personal character.
While he preaches up faith alone, in our justification
before God, he is careful to maintain good works. These
things the grace of God teaches us. And how much of
this doctrine has he transcribed into his life! How rich
has he been in all good works! What an eminent pat-
tern of piety towards God? How holy and unblameable
in all conversation and godliness! How seasoned, how
much to the use of edifying all his discourses! How na-
turally does he turn them to religion! How much is he

given to devotion himself, and how much does he
to excite it in others!

It is indisputable with me, that he affects no par
religion, nor sets himself at the head of any. He i
bigotted to the lesser rites and forms of religion, i
zealous enough in all its essentials. He professes le
good men of every denomination. His heart seem
upon doing good. He goes about his great Ma
work with diligence and application, and with such el
fulness as would make one in love with a life of reli
He is proof against reproach and invective. When
reviled, he revileth not again; but prays heartily fe
his enemies.

He renders to all their due; while zealous for the t
of God, is a friend to Cæsar. And for charity, as it
sists in compassion, and acts of beneficence we have
men like minded. Had he been under any crimin
fluence of a mercenary temper—had he collected m
for himself in his journies, under the pretext of do.
for the poor, as he was slanderously reported, he
certainly a fair opportunity to enrich himself. Bo
have seen, and plain fact cannot be denied, that he
all into the treasury, and serves the tables of the
with it. Strolling and vagabond orphans, without fi
and without mother, without purse and without fr
he seeks out, picks up, and adopts into his family. I
now building accommodations, and laying the best i
dation for their support and maintenance.

I now proceed to give my opinion what views P
dence may have in raising up men of this stamp.

And this I desire to do with all humility and modes

I pretend to no spirit of prophecy, and can only
jecture, and offer the result of observation, reason,
the usual tendencies of things, corroborated by the
promises scattered up and down in our Bibles.

Now we are none of us ignorant, how far the prim
spirit of Christianity has sunk into a mere form of g
ness: irreligion has been rushing in like a flood; the
est and most obvious doctrines of the Bible fallen into
contempt: the principles and systems of our pious fat
have been more and more exploded. And now
seems to have revived the ancient spirit and doctr
He is raising up of our young men with zeal and cou
to stem the torrent. They have preached with

assiduity and success, such solemn awe have they
k upon their hearers.   Such deep convictions have
sermons produced: so much have they roused and
ed the zeal of ministers and people: so intrepidly do
push through all opposition.   It looks as if some
y period were opening."

such accounts as these, many ministers and people
excited to desire his assistance in carrying on that
al of religion, which, some years before, was begun
ne parts of our land, and were prepared to embrace

THE END.

Printed by BoD™in Norderstedt, Germany

9 781527 629806